# The Frog Who Dreamed She Was an Opera Singer

# The Frog Who Dreamed She Was an Opera Singer

## JACKIE KAY

*Illustrated by*
**Sue Williams**

BLOOMSBURY
CHILDREN'S
BOOKS

*For Matthew with love*

First published in Great Britain in 1998
Bloomsbury Publishing Plc, 38 Soho Square, London, W1V 5DF

A CIP catalogue record of this book is available from the
British Library

ISBN 0 7475 3866 2

Printed in England by Clays Ltd, St Ives plc

10 9 8 7 6 5 4 3 2 1

# Contents

# The Hole Story

You sure you want the whole story?
All right, you got the hole story.
I was born tiny, mendable
in the smelly sock of Will MacDowall.

Soon, I was the dark sweet cavity
in the slippy mouth of Lisa MacVittie.
But Hey, I had high holes for myself.
Fuelled by ambition, I craved big roles.

I was a hole for a mole, a mouse, a man,
a key, a button, a spy, a can.
I lived through holes, peeping and weeping,
happy holes, sad holes, big holes, deep in.

You name them; I've been them – Polo,
mint. Loads of good parts playing solo.
I've been a hole in a halo, hole in a doughnut.
I've aimed high and low, meant a hole lot, but

I've been all holes to all people.
Pupil, nostril, earhole, unmentionable!
Had cheesy days in Emmental cheese,
gooey days in honeycombs from bees.

I've picked a hole and made it holy,
the secret lagoon, the tearful valley.
I've played every role a hole can play:
snooker, basketball, golf – got a birdie.

The sudden shock of the hard white ball,
the thrill-swoop of the basketball.
O there was nothing I hadn't seen;
there was no hole I hadn't been.

That was my downhole. I wanted to be bigger
    and bigger.
Till before I could say *Hallelujah*
I was the black hole; then the hole in the earth.
The saddest hole in the whole world is the
    hole in the earth.

I am the abyss. You can't a void me.
Hear my howl of anguish. Stop me.
I didn't mean to get so out of control.
O to be a wee hole!

O to be a wee hole!
To go back to Will MacDowall's
woolly, grey, smelly sock.
O to turn back the clock!

## Duane's Fillings

Duane is famous in our school.
He's got thirteen fillings.
Duane doesn't bother with football.
All day he stands by the railings

showing off his silver fillings.
His mouth open wide and appalling.
Somebody, starstruck, counts them.
Duane's got a story for each one.

He's had his fillings out.
And's he's had them put back in.
It's nobody's business
how many times Duane's been to the dentist.

One came out in a toffee.
One came out in a pink bubblegum.
Duane doesn't call them fillings.
He calls them amalgums.

'Why did you need so many?' we say.
'It shouldn't be necessary.'
'Too many apples when I was little,'
says Duane, without a smile.

'That's not right,' says Dwight.
'Don't be silly,' says Billy.
'Nah,' says Jah.
'Sweets make your teeth rotten!'

'Too many sweets,' says Pete.
Duane says, 'I know what I know.'
And smiles a big silver smile.
'Too many *toffee* apples.'

## Mr and Mrs Lilac

Never go to the Lilac's house
to fetch back your ball.
The Lilacs don't like children.
They don't like children at all.

Mr and Mrs Lilac steal children's balls.
They've got mine, they've got my pals'.
Mr Lilac loathes you ringing his bell.
He says, 'It's my ball now, my ball.'

Mr Lilac smiles a terrible smile.
He watches you shake and tremble.
Mrs Lilac says, 'It's our land dear.'
'Our land. You should be careful.'

Once I peeped through their window.
The moon shone on my shadow.
Inside the Lilacs were playing ball.
There was haunting music in the hall.

An orange light glowed in the room.
Their faces were bright as broom.
Mr Lilac passed Mrs Lilac my basketball.
Mrs Lilac passed Mr Lilac Mugsy's rugby ball.

The strange thing was all our balls
looked new again, through the window.
Lisa's leather football, still bright white.
Django's tennis ball, garish yellow tonight.

Nasreen's new golf balls, Jodie's bouncy balls,
Billy's baseballs, Pili's ping-pong balls.
I heard Mrs Lilac laugh through the window.
'Good throw, Mr Lilac, Good throw.'

# The Christmas Burglar

So,
dressed up as usual,
I'm standing behind the window –
laughing lights, silver tinsel,
tiny Santas and chocolate bells,
and, just for show, an angel –
serene at my peak,
Meek.
Breathless presents surrounding me,
keeping their wild secrets under wraps, dying,
just dying, to be ripped open. Oh! I was in a brilliant mood.
I knew I looked good. When the brick came crashing through, Ah-Ah,
when the window gave out sharp yells of pane, Yaa-bang!
when the man broke into our warm room,
wearing thick black gloves, spreading doom,
I was so frightened, I dropped my pines.
One by one, my fine needles lost their green nerves.
I shook. I trembled. My bells fell off. My tinsel crawled, slithered
behind the couch. My lights went out. But worst, worst of all.
The man took my presents, from under me! Ripped them open,
bagged what he fancied. He made scary noises.
Grunting. Eyes glinting.
He swore a lot. When he liked something,
he whistled softly to himself.
The worst sound in the world.
The whole room was a total mess. Plant-mud on the carpet.
Shattered glass. Talk about distress! Never seen the like of it.
I was so helpless. My sparkling, glittering, shining, presents.
Christmas! Would you believe? Christmas Eve, Eve, Eve.
I can do nothing except dread the morning.
When the children come running down with their excited
feet,what am I supposed to say?
Santa has been and gone
A burglar's been and gone.
Have a good one!
**Merry Xmas!**
**Merry Xmas!**
**Merry Xmas!**

## What the Dog Did on November the 5<sup>th</sup>

Here we go again! Sulphur in the air again.
Vicious bangs, violent skies again.
Lightning bugs, luminous fireflies.
The thick fog of gunpowder. Grrrrrrr.
It is not a pretty picture.
It's a dog's exploding nightmare.
And Woof! I feel sorry for the Guy.
I'm a dog that likes a quiet life –
Hush puppies, a book of poetry,
all curled up, a dog-eared book of doggerel.
I know myself so well.
So, this year I decides
I am not taking it lying down.
I refuse to be a basket-case one more time.
So dogs, all dogs, big tails and wee tails,
show-offs and cowards, pedigrees and
    mongrels,
Get a load of this:
This year I've a plot up my paw
worthy of the great Mr Fawkes himself!
No more skulking under the table
tail stuck between my shaking legs.
No clutching at the baby in the cot

with my soft padded paws
as one gunpowder applause after another
sweeps the booming, trembling sky.
No guys and girls. No flame tails.
I won't be wishing I was dead as a dog-nail.
Or barking my most heartbreaking piteous bark,
my most hellish Hound of the Baskerville bark
Whooooo Whooooooo
    Whoooooooooooooooooooooooooooo.
(Head thrown back for special effects.)
No, no, no, my comrades. None of that.
This November the 5th I won't watch
my mistress light a Mount Vesuvius
and rush, the bum's rush, back to safety.
Or the children's sparkling sizzling faces.
Enough is enough is enough is enough.
Ruff. Ruff. Ruff.
Let sleeping dogs lie!
This is my dark night, ma noche.
Whoooooooo Whoooooo Whooooooooooooooo.
From the second I clocked those nasty boxes
hit my local newsagents, I was on the case.
Red alert. Orange alert. Blue alert.
So when my mistress placed our box
in the cubbyhole under the stairs,

I opened it and took them out,
one by one: Yellow Zodiac, Jack in the Box,
Catherine Wheel, Emerald Cascade, Dragon's
    Crown,
and went on down
to the back of my back garden
and buried them, one by one,
next to my favourite oldest bone.
Well. When she went to the cubby-hole
and found a big empty box,
not a sizzler in sight;
when the children stared to whine and moan
Awwwwwwwwwwwww Awwwwww
    Owwwwwww Owwwwwwwwwwwwww.
When they barked that's not fair,
Get us some more,
when I heard her say,
'explosives are too expensive',
I couldn't keep it in.
I just couldn't keep it in.
I grabbed my mistress by the sleeve
and rushed fast as a rocket
to the scene of my crime,
where one by one I dug them up:
Harlequin, Firefly, Carnival Spray.
Shooting Star. Mount Etna. Giant Rocket.
All totally, hopelessly wet,

saturated in soaking mud.
The kids shouted 'You naughty dog!!!'
into my long ear. I was in the doghouse all right.
But I had no shame. Never fear.
And strangely enough I've become famous.
I'm a national celebrity.
My bright idea caught alight.
Everyone was at it in a few years.
Digging plots and planting rockets.
Wagging tails. Now, every November the 5th
up and down the breadth of the country,
the Irish terriers, Scottish terriers,
English ones and Welsh ones,
gather in the dark night
and let out one bonfire bark of sheer delight.
All because of a smart dog like me.
I am nobody's dogsbody.
Whoooooooooooo Whoooooooooooooooooooooo.
  Whooooo ooooooo.

# Jimmy Mush

Well there once was a boy by the name of
   Jimmy
MUSH.
When he walked into a full room under a full
   moon,
everyone shouted: 'Hush, Hush it's Jimmy
MUSH.'
Sammy rushed to bring Jimmy
MUSH
his chair, and he sat there,
combing his dark hair under the full glare of
   the moon,
and ate his food with a silver spoon.

He was lush was Jimmy
MUSH.
Black curly hair, brown skin, the longest
   eyelash.
Always a kind word to say: Good Morning,
   Good Day.
Never pretended he didn't see you or run
   away did Jimmy
MUSH.
Never did push forward in a queue, or make
   you feel blue.

Never did say, 'I don't have a clue.'
He'd sing to you from his sash windows
    would Jimmy
MUSH.

And the people in the street below would
    shout, 'Shush, Shush
It's Jimmy
MUSH!'
The people looked up at Jimmy behind his
    sash,
then everybody gushed, 'Oh Jimmy
MUSH.'
His singing was uplifting. (Gregorian
    chanting.)
Suddenly, to the astonishment of everybody
    including Jimmy
MUSH
The whole crowd started to levitate,

Till they were floating higher than their pash.
    And Jimmy
MUSH
looked up from his white sash
and saw the crowd screaming from the
    clouds.
So he sang a low note, a deeply dark low note,

Oh-Oh, Oh-Oh,
  OOOOOOOOOOOO000000000000H,
Till they all came bump-bumping down.
Bum, Bum, Bum, Bum,
  Bummmmmmmmmmmmmmmmmmmmm.
From that day to this day, and on, Jimmy
MUSH

Could raise dosh, I mean lots of it, cash,
for any good cause, singing HIGH to raise the
  people
and LOW to bring them down.
Well, the crowd got bigger by the year, and
  Jimmy
MUSH
raised a lavish amount of cash, till one day he
  just

got bored. Too much adulation and
   admiration.
He wouldn't sing and he wouldn't wash;
and he changed his name from Jimmy
MUSH

To . . . but that would be telling, so Hush,
   Hush.

PS:
You might suggest another name for Jimmy
MUSH

## The Frog Who Dreamed She Was an Opera Singer

There once was a frog
who dreamed she was an opera singer.
She wished so hard she grew a long throat
and a beautiful polkadot green coat
and intense opera singer's eyes.
She even put on a little weight.
But she couldn't grow tall.
She just couldn't grow tall.
She leaped to the Queen Elizabeth Hall,
practising her aria all the way.
Her voice was promising and lovely.
She couldn't wait to leapfrog on to the stage.
What a presence on the stage!
All the audience in the Queen Elizabeth Hall,
gasped to see one so small sing like that.
Her voice trembled and swelled
and filled with colour.
That frog was a green prima donna.

# Innit

Innit he's a football star, my dad.
Innit he's got a gold car, my dad.
Innit, he dresses really bad, my dad.
Innit, his muscles are well hard, my dad.
Innit, he's got a sixpack, my dad.
Innit, he's the leader of his pack, my dad.
Innit, his flying kick is wild, my dad.
Innit, I'm his only child, my dad.
Innit, he's rich and famous, my dad.

Innit, I've been had, my dad.
Innit, I've never met him, my dad.
Innit, he's bought me nothing, my dad.
Innit, I've got his eyes, my dad.
(I hope I haven't caught his lies, my dad.)
Innit, I'm not rich and famous.
I'm not, am I? Innit? Innit? Innit?

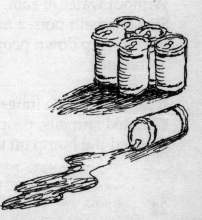

## Sulk Pod

The place was the Sahara desert,
the heat, dust, everything inert,
where the seed of sulk grew into Sulk Pod;

and my God, Sulk Pod was Something!
It was the colour of an aubergine.
It had thick, heavy skin. Saturnine.

It glowered and growled and grumbled.
It swelled in sultry acid soil.
The size of a zit, a pluke, a boil.

Without water or rain, Sulk Pod grew.
Size of a petit pois, a mange tout. It knew
How to slip down people's throats, under
    tongues.

It headed for the lungs. The heart.
Claimed animals, people.
Created the hump on the back of the camel.

The sulky slime of the snail.
The sulky ears of the Spaniel.
It took over landscapes as well.

The swamp, the salt marsh, the bog,
the sulky sea, the sea fog.
Sulk Pod was out there seizing

the sea creatures; the shrimp, the shell fish,
the clam, the crayfish,
the mussel, the whelk, the mollusc.

Sulk Pod could eliminate smiles.
A grinning girl – Pod! – into a grouchy girl.
A friendly old face – Pod! – into a jowl-scowl.

Suddenly, millions were taking the hump,
off in the cream puff, down in the dumps,
cheesed off, browned off, beyond belief,

Counting grumbles, giving it grief;
all put out and chip on the shoulder.
Sulk Pod could transform the sky's temper –

Till the grey clouds swirled and stewed
till storm on the long face bubbled and
    brewed
till the mustard purse of the mouth

opened and snapped shut,
and the lips petted, giving it Big Pout,
and the slow sulker, stung, crept up the stairs
  like a thief,

the insult as big as belief,
and pulled the sulky covers over the sulky
  head,
and at the unfairness of it
  all, wept in bed.

## The Very Irritating Person

I am a very irritating person, Ducks.
I've been told this, so I'm afraid it's true.
I spend half an hour in the loo.
I blow my nose loudly; I do scary At-tish-
    shoos.
I tut-tut-tut like a kangaroo.
When I knock at a door, I shout 'You-Who?'
I play tricks in the nervous person's house.
I shout 'Mouse! Mouse!' Then, 'just joking!'
I'm a nit-picker. I like exact figures.
If someone protests, I say, 'Oh Please!'
I snore: an extremely original snore,
half-way between choking and dying.
I walk slowly in front of quick people
who bump into me and say 'Sorry' furiously –
'*Saw-RRY!*' I say 'The fault is all mine.'
I apologise profusely,
for tiny faults or major personality defects
    equally.
I smile an irritating range of smiles –
from the hint of a smile,
to the toothy goofy mile of a smile.
I smile if someone is shouting at me.
Patronising, cheesy, head to the one side.
'That's very sad. Tuttuttut.What a pity.'

I am so irritating, I irritate myself occasionally.
Tetchy Tetchy Tetchy! Well well well.
If I really want to drive people up the wall,
I'll say things three times, whistle between my
    teeth,
do my wild giggle. 'But, but, but,' I interrupt,
until someone screams: 'WHAT!'
And I say, 'Oh nothing really.
I can't remember what I was about to say.'
Then I rub my hands (partly in glee)
because my dears, don't you see?
– that for every irritating person like me,
there is an irritated person,
whose goat is easy to get,
whose teeth are easy to set
on edge, whose nose is easy to get
up, whose skin is easy to get
under, whose face goes red or blotchy
in any random attack of irritability.
If I had to choose, my ducks, my pets,
between being irritating or irritable,
there's no contest, my chickadees.
Being an irritating person
is infinitely preferable. Oh Please!

## Pomegranate
(*For Chorlton Park School*)

See, if it hadnie been for Persephone,
you'd have thought someone
was having you on
when you first clapped eyes on:
snow, a bald tree, yellow grass,
or happened to pass
a snowman in a field of frost,
or an icicle hanging from a sash-
windie, or bare roses, lashing sleet or slush.

You'd have never failed an exam,
because you simply wouldnie have gone
to school. You'd have had summer holidays
– a summer holiday symphony always –
if Persephone had clocked the Golden Rule,
and kept her beautiful lips sealed;
if she had not sucked those six small reds,
down in the deep dark world of the dead,
where every tree had lost its big head.

Next time someone offers you a wee bite of
    fruit –
think seriously for a second, then scoot.

## Black Ann

They call me Black Ann all the way up the
  Mississippi.
They call me Black Ann all the way up the
  Mississippi.
I cook on the Mississippi steamboat, everyone
  knows me.
I been many big places, but my heart's in
  Missouri.

When I think of Missouri, I think of my son
  Billy.
My son Billy in Missouri without his own
  Mammy.
Is he sleeping at night, no mammy singin
  sweetly?
He's workin' for the bossman even tho' he's
  just a pickney.

At night when the steamboat takes me down
the Mississippi,
I get to thinkin' 'bout Billy, all I do is worry.
Tired of cookin', I get too tired to do any
sleepin',
It's Billy in the mornin'; it's Billy in the
evenin'.

They call me Black Ann all the way up the
Mississippi.
Everybody knows my steamboat, praises my
cookin' highly.
When I get enough money, I'm buying back
my Billy.
The bossman he done told me, he cost a pretty
penny.

Five hundred dollars to buy me back my own
   son Billy.
Well every meal I make is a meal for my sweet
   Billy.
Every mouthful they take is a mouthful for
   my boy.
One day I'll buy my Billy way down in that
   Missouri.

It's been three long years since I set eyes on
   my Billy.
I'm praying Billy's not forgotten his good old
   mammy.
I'm gonna be a big surprise one day in
   Missouri.
I'm gonna havta say 'Billy son, I'm your own
   mammy.

They call me Black Ann all the way up the
   Mississippi.'

## At Home, Abroad

All summer
I dream of
places I've never
been
where I might
see faces
I've never seen,
like the dark
face of my
father in
Nigeria,
or the pale
face of my
mother in
the Highlands,
or the bright
faces of my
cousins at
Land's End.

All summer
I spell the names
of tricky countries
just in case
I get a sudden

invite: Madagascar,
Cameroon. I draw
cartoons of
airports, big and small.
Who will meet me?
Will they
shake hands or
kiss both cheeks?
I draw
duty frees
with every
country's favourite
sweetie, smiling
a sugary welcome,
and myself,
cap-peaked,
wondering if I am
'home'.

## Ferry Tale

The Tobermoray Ferry brings us in from
　　Oban.
The snappy seagulls steal bread from my
　　hands.
My mother sings 'The Isle of Mull' over and
　　over
holding me close in my brown anorak on the
　　North Sea.

Off the ferry, the local people gather around
　　me.
They cluck and stare and ask my mother,
'Does she have the English? Does she have the
　　English?'
My mother takes my brown hand in hers by
　　the North Sea.

## The Past

The girl I was is out at sea.
Isn't that funny? She just walks
further and further away, slowly.

Soon I'll think we had different lives
me and her, her and me.
Maybe I'll wave to her across the sea,

lift my arm high above my shoulder
and wave to the wee girl with the black curly hair,
her skirt way above her knees in the dark sea.

## Summer Romance

I was best friends with Sabah
the whole long summer;
I admired her handwriting,
the way she smiled into
the summer evening,
her voice, melted butter.
The way her chin shone
under a buttercup.
Everyone let Sabah
go first in a long
hot summer queue.
The way she always looked
fancy, the way
she said 'Fandango',
and plucked her banjo;
her big purple bangle
banged at her wrist;
her face lit by the angle
poise lamp in her room,
her hair all a tangle,
damp from the summer heat,
Sabah's eyes sparkled all summer.

But when the summer was gone
and the winter came,

in walked Big Heather Murphy.
Sabah turned her lovely head
towards her. I nearly died.
Summer holidays burn with lies.

## Word of a Lie

I am the fastest runner in my school and that's
NO WORD OF A LIE
I've got gold fillings in my teeth and that's
NO WORD OF A LIE
In my garden, I've got my own big bull and
that's
NO WORD OF A LIE
I'm brilliant at giving my enemies grief and
that's
NO WORD OF A LIE
I can multiply 3 billion and twenty-seven by
nine billion four thousand and one in two
seconds and that's
NO WORD OF A LIE
I can calculate the distance between the
planets before you've had toast
And that's
NO WORD OF A LIE
I can always tell when my best pals boast and
that's
NO WORD OF A LIE

I'd been round the world twice before I was
   three and a quarter and that's
NO WORD OF A LIE
I am definitely my mother's favourite
   daughter and that's
NO WORD OF A LIE
I am brilliant at witches' laughter and
   that's
NO WORD OF A LIE
I can tell the weather from one look at the sky
   and that's
NO WORD OF A LIE
I can predict disasters, floods, earthquakes
   and murders and that's
NO WORD OF A LIE
I can always tell when other people lie and
   that's
NO WORD OF A LIE
I can even tell if someone is going to die and
   that's
NO WORD OF A LIE
I am the most popular girl in my entire school
   and that's
NO WORD OF A LIE
I know the golden rule, don't play the fool,
   don't boast, be shy and that's
NO WORD OF A LIE

I am sensitive, I listen, I have kind brown eyes
    and that's
NO WORD OF A LIE

You don't believe me, do you?
ALL RIGHT, ALL RIGHT, ALL RIGHT
I am the biggest liar in my school and that's
NO WORD OF A LIE

## Stressed Out

I am totally stressed out.
I can't sleep at night.
I shake when I hear them shout.
He has his nerve pills; she has her alcohol.

Me? I have nothing at all.
There is no one to talk to.
I have this strange singing in my head.
At night, alone in bed,

The stress is in my sheets,
clinging to my nightdress,
climbing in through the windows.
There are tests tomorrow;

bullies posted in the playground.
Many things to remember.
I told my mother: I said,
'I am totally stressed out.'

She said, 'Don't be silly
Children don't get stressed.'
'Like Hell they don't,' I said.
And she sent me to my room for swearing.

So now here I am,
stuck in my stupid bedroom,
locked up, stressed out, all alone.
I swear to bring my stress levels down.

Life sucks.

## Astrorat

The rat overheard someone say:
rats have followed man everywhere,
through the plague, off the sinking ship,
but they haven't gone to the moon,
oh no, a rat has never gone to the moon.

This was one ambitious rat
who felt rattled to hear about the moon.
The moon that looked like a huge cheese.
The stars, like tiny bright mice.
The rat spent the next fortnight searching

for an astronaut and a space rocket.
At last, he found one in Russia;
he was over the moon with joy.
Astrorat scuttled into the man's provisions,
crossed his rat legs for the countdown,
and squealed a huge rat squeal of satisfaction

when that rocket took off for the moon.

# Barbie For Life

Barbie, my Barbie is no ordinary doll.
She is the doll to end dolls.
She is the life and soul.
You couldn't dump her for another doll.

A girl that gives up on Barbie
deserves to die. That's no lie.

True she is cute. She is shapely.
But she is as jealous as Hell.
She is definitely no modest doll.
I warn you! Neglect her at your peril.

A girl that gives up on Barbie
deserves to die. That's no lie.

Try and chuck Barbie and she'll be back.
You'll think you're on your own,
then you'll hear a soft knock-knock-knock.
She'll follow you with her quick feet.

A girl that gives up on Barbie
deserves to die. That's no lie.

She will not tolerate excuses.
Your last moments will not impress.
You will be put under terrible duress.
Barbie has no mercy for girls like you.

A girl that gives up on Barbie
deserves to die. That's no lie.

Don't be fickle. Don't be a cheat.
Or you'll find you are shredded meat.
Barbie means Barbie for life.
So let me tell you quickly, take my advice.

(I don't think she's eavesdropping.)
Go and get yourself a teddy or someone nice.
Or else you will be stuck with Barbie for ever.
Oh God. She heard me. I'm done for.

Aaaaaaaaah.

## The Sick Bed

The sick bed was sick to death of itself.
Pillows feathery with delusions,
the pale white sheet shivering in the thin
   night,
the moaning mattress muttering in the early
   morning,
the bed frame calling everybody for
   everything,
making bad things up about good friends,
delirious, shouting.

The glass beside the sick bed, drained.
The bottle of medicine, feverish red.
The tissues sneezing in their own box.
The sick bed got hotter and hotter,
till the wooden frame started to sweat,
till it longed for a bucket of ice-cold water,
till it longed for a mother.

*Mummy's here, mummy's here*, said the voice in
   the room

but the sick bed did not believe her,
Mummy was nowhere to be seen or felt.
The sick bed was all alone in the room,
weeping on its weak wooden legs,
'Get me, Get me, Get me!' shouted the sick
  bed. 'Quick!'

One morning, the air was suddenly light
in the sick room, the gloom disappeared.
The sun breathed in, yellow and bright.
The child rose from the sick bed, stood
on ginger legs, shaking a cool head.
One fresh morning it was wonderful to realise
that the child was no longer a bed,
that the terrible voice in the head was dead.

# Miss Always Believes Christopher

Miss always believes Christopher.
Miss doesn't believe anybody else but
    Christopher.
He can do no wrong even when he does
    wrong.
Her eyes are full of glitter for Christopher.

His every word is a precious stone.
He is loved by Miss and cherished by Miss.
The rest of us are on our own.
Miss always believes Christopher.

If ever there are two versions of a story,
Miss will always believe Christopher's.
His is the special seat, the glory.
The one who can never be naughty.

It's not as if Christopher is clever.
It's not as if he is good at Maths.
He never brought nothing for the Tombola.
But Miss always believes Christopher.

Miss believes Christopher so much
That I've started believing him too.
Christopher is my best friend and as such,
I wish Miss would believe me too.

## Girl Footballer

The ball soars and the ball flies.
The ball goes up. The ball goes in.
And the balls in your eyes
are rolling and spinning,
spinning and rolling.
And the blood in your heart is singing.

You feel yourself whirl and twirl.
What a talented girl.
Nothing like this feeling you get
when the ball bulges in the back of the net.
No, you don't easily forget
the sweet sweet taste of a goal.
Replay it in your mind again:

Left foot in the air, flick,
straight to the back of the net.
Play it again and again
– the ball's beautiful roll to the goal.
Nothing like the soaring and roaring
when the plump ball hits the thin net.
And the sad blue goalie sits on the sad green grass.
The look on the slow face,

watching the ball go past, fast.
No chance. No chance. Watching the ball dance.
You dribble from the midfield down.
You get past three men.
You do a chip, a volley, you curl the ball.
You perm the air with your talent, and all
the fans sizzle and spark,
all the fans sing and dance,
football is one long romance
with the ball, with the ball and all.

You nutmeg the goalie like the goalie is a spice.
You get the ball in, not once, twice, but thrice!
Hat trick! You make the goalie feel sick.
So you lie down and roll in celebration.
You feel the team jump on your back
then you feel the whole nation,
goggle-eyed in admiration.
You squeeze your fist,
like this, like a kiss, to the wild crowd
and your football of a heart is bouncing and proud.

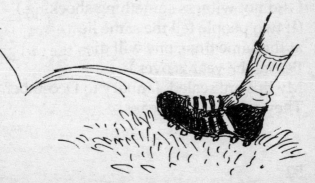

## No-Speaks

I am the child who stopped talking
Three years ago. There was heavy snow.
It was a blow to my family, I know.
They call me No-Speaks.
It has been one hundred and fifty-six weeks
Since I came to my decision about speech.
I clocked it was a waste of time,
to talk in plain speech or rhyme.
So, I watch the telling hands chime.
I watch the trees grow big beards, fuzzy hair.
Then, I watch them get alopecia.
I watch the snow melt into summer.
I hold my tongue round the clock.
They call me No-Speaks.
I shut my mouth from season to season.
I have a very good reason,
For never saying a single word.
Not a single dickie bird.
(I was not struck by lightning.
I did not witness something shocking.)
(If two people tell the same lie
at the same time, one will die
Before the year is over.)
My lips are sealed, January to December.
They call me No-Speaks.

I am a closed book. A sealed letter.
A shut letter-box.
I despise the blether, the chatterbox.
Since I shut my trap,
Life is much better.
But every sound is an electric shock.
Leaves are shy when they first
fall from trees.

## WordPerfect

In the stinking dark hole
in the middle of the wild woods
the fox received a fax.

In the outbacks of Australia
near the aboriginal's river
the emu got an e-mail.

In the middle of the Atlantic ocean
in the cold mid-winter,
the fish went on the Net.

In the wooden shanty house
in the shanty town
the spider got on the Web.

In the highlands of Scotland
by the tall Scots pine trees
the ram loaded ram.

Scuttling across the desert
in the desperate heat,
the mouse clicked the mouse.

Running across the prairies
for the first time,
the floppy foal got a file.

In the smelly stinky barn of a small dairy
    farm,
the hen wrote with a quill pen,
the secret of the universe.

## Tommy MacCormack

I was a good boy who needed a bad boy –
Tommy MacCormack.
Just the sound of his name made me bounce
my ball on the tarmac.
Tommy MacCormack.
My voice was different to his;
his was dirt and dust and slack,

mine was high and squeaky clean.
I wished I could change my name to
Tommy MacCormack.
He said rude words, awful rude words,
I sucked till the colour changed on my tongue –
Shite! Swine! Or even the F word.
Tommy and his wide slow grin.

Nobody dared lift a finger to me,
when I was with Tommy MacCormack,
nor call me swot or thwack my back;
he had a real knack of making everyone do as
    he said
did Tommy MacCormack.
He played me smoochy musak, Womack and
    Womack,
ran his fingers down the length of my back,
did a moonie round his wild room,
lit a Regal, flicked his fringe,
then did what he did best, my bad boy,
my Tommy MacCormack.

## Chatterbox

Oh, I like talking, me.
There's so much to say,
so much to enthuse about.
Isn't life fascinating?
Isn't it just the bees knees?
'When do you NOT talk?'
people ask me. But what
is the point in keeping schtum,
in being glum and gossipless?
I'm one of those people
that celebrates the tongue
the vocal cords, the voice box.
I've got some pair of lungs.
Imagine the day the first tongue crawled
into the first mouth!
What a big pink thick day that was.
My own tongue is a bit long
and a bit spongy for my liking;
but let's face it,
I couldn't chatter without it.
I couldn't gossip or natter or whitter.
Couldn't spread rumours, have a slanging match
a chinwag, a heart-to-heart, a tête-à-tête.
I bet I couldn't hold a debate,
articulate or enunciate,

imitate or communicate, could I?
Then I wouldn't be a Blether of Hell
or a chatterbox, would I?
Somebody once said,
THEY SHOULD CUT OUT YOUR TONGUE.
That hurt my feelings.
I cried.
But even when I was crying,
I couldn't stop talking.
That's sob not sob fair sob, said I.
SHUT UP, said the coarse voice,
and worse – BUTTON IT.
I ran to my room,
whispered to my mirror.
The girl in there was cool, kind.
But her eyes were red from crying.
I said to her, Aw, don't cry so.
You're just a chatterbox.
Just a bit loquacious.
But I love you to bits.
She smiled, the girl in the glass.
I ran down the stairs to grant forgiveness.
It's important to grant forgiveness
now and again, not too often.
Don't you agree?
Oh, I like talking, me.

# The Living Photograph

My small grandmother is tall there,
straight-back, white broderie anglaise shirt,
pleated skirt, flat shoes, grey bun,
a kind, old smile round her eyes.
Her big hand holds mine,
white hand in black hand.
Her sharp blue eyes look her own death in the
    eye.

It was true afterall; that look.
My tall grandmother became small.
Her back round and hunched.
Her soup forgot to boil.
She went to the awful place grandmothers go.
Somewhere unknown, unthinkable.

But there she is still,
in the photo with me at three,
the crinkled smile is still living, breathing.

## Grandpa's Soup

No one makes soup like my Grandpa's,
with its diced carrots the perfect size
and its diced potatoes the perfect size
and its wee soft bits –
what are their names?
and its big bit of hough,
which rhymes with loch, floating
like a rich island in the middle of the soup sea.

I say, Grandpa, Grandpa your soup is the best
    soup in the whole world.
And Grandpa says, Och,
which rhymes with hough and loch,
Och, Don't be daft,
because he's shy about his soup, my Grandpa.
He knows I will grow up and pine for it.
I will fall ill and desperately need it.
I will long for it my whole life after he is gone.
Every soup will become sad and wrong after
    he is gone.

He knows when I'm older I will avoid soup
  altogether.
Oh Grandpa, Grandpa, why is your soup so
  glorious? I say
tucking into my fourth bowl in a day.

Barley! That's the name of the wee soft bits.
  Barley.

## Matthew Dreams of Chinchillas

When his eyes close in his bedroom
and his covers are snug round his shoulders,
when his light is out
and darkness falls,
Matthew dreams of Chinchillas.
There are two of them,
four chocolate eyes,
four cute round ears listening out for him.
And in his room in the deep dark night,
no harm can ever come to him.
When the puff-padded feet
in the furry moonlight
are warm on the palm of his hand,
and he wakes from the dream
one snowy morning
to find his own self staring –
deep, deep, deeper still
into the real,
kind dark eye of Chinchilla;
then he looks in the mirror,
and his own eyes are the very same colour.

# BLOOMSBURY CHILDREN'S
# POETRY TITLES

ISBN 0 7475 3866 2

The Frog
who dreamed she was an
Opera Singer

ISBN 0 7475 3864 6

The World's your
Lobster
ADRIAN HENRI

ISBN 0 7475 3865 4

once upon an
animal

ISBN 0 7475 3863 8

ROBOCAT
ADRIAN HENRI